Theta & the Lost Slipper

Written & Illustrated by Alycia D'Avino

Published by
Moon Goddess Studio

Text copyright © 2022 Alycia D'Avino
Illustrations copyright © 2022 Alycia D'Avino

All rights reserved.
This book, or parts thereof, may not be reproduced in any form without permission in writing from the publisher.
The scanning, uploading and distribution of this book via the internet or via any other means
without permission from the publisher is illegal and punishable by law.

This is a work of fiction. Any resemblance or likeness to any person or event is purely coincidence.

This book is printed on demand wherever our printer deems it necessary.
Most or all orders in the U.S.A. will be printed in the U.S.A.

Hardcover ISBN: 979-8-218-00057-8

Published by

www.moongoddeessstudio.com

Book designed in partnership with

NONESPOT™
PUBLISHING

www.nonespot.com

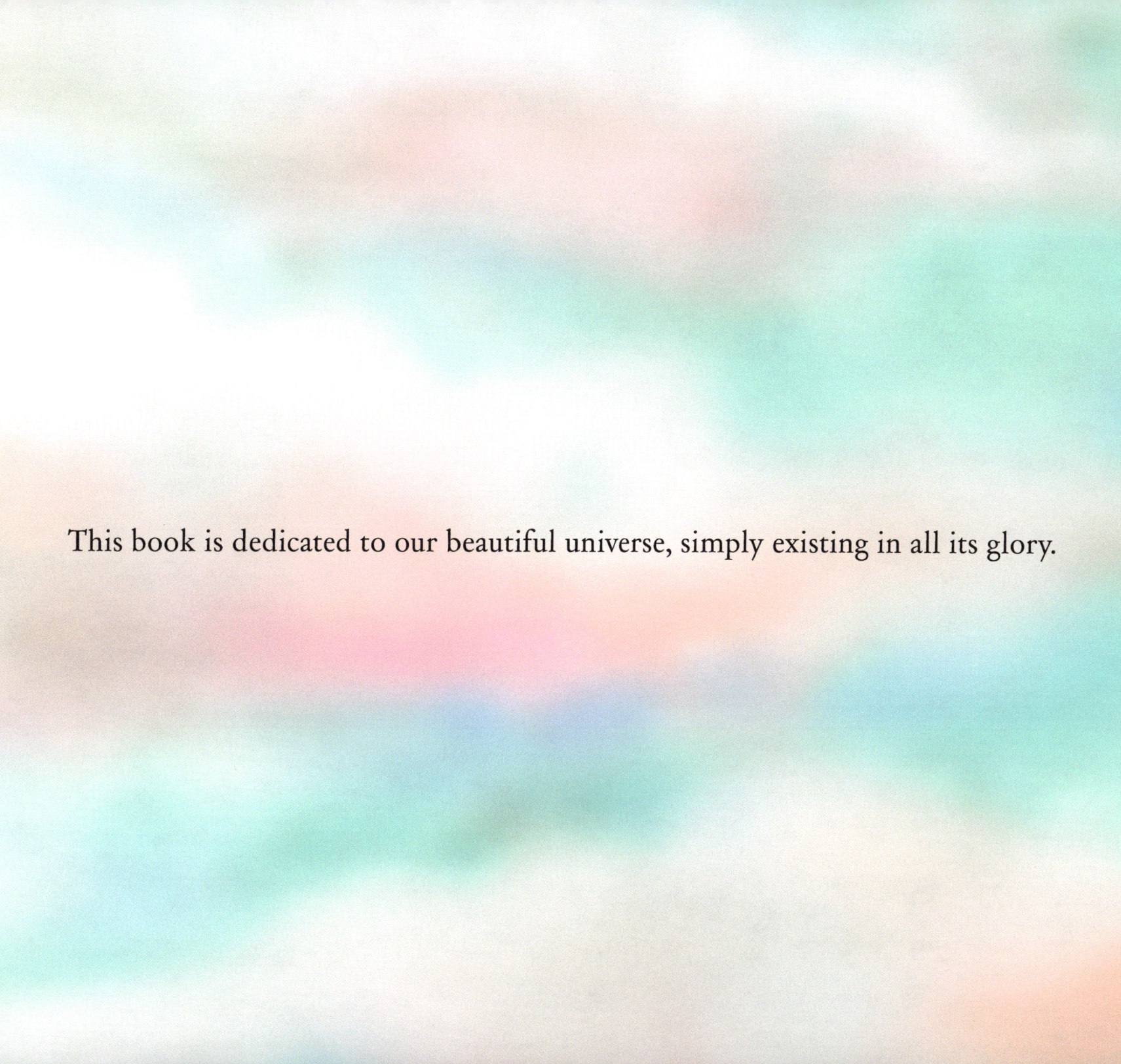

This book is dedicated to our beautiful universe, simply existing in all its glory.

Before the dawn of days and the fall of nights, there lived a girl named Theta, who all of a sudden, in one moment, found herself sinking into a world of time.

She did not know what this world would bring, just as she did not know what came before. She only knew that she was there, right then, in that very moment, somewhere in time.

Down below she sank, somewhere, out there, into the deep blue.
The blue surrounded her, carried her gently all the way down,
but kept her slipper on the way.

A tear fell from Theta's cheek as she saw her slipper disappear, lost into the blue.

As she reached the bottom, a creature appeared.

"Don't cry traveler," said the creature.
"Much will be lost here and plenty will be found,
this world of time is full of treasures and thieves,
some to be seen and others unseen.
It is not without loss that something can be found."

And with those words, the creature was gone,
leaving only the sound of Theta and time.
Tick - Tock - Tear Drop - as one by one Theta's tears became the blue.

Eventually, their song began to fade and Theta's tears stopped.
It was then that a green light appeared from above illuminating
a treasure she had been sitting beside.

The sight of the treasure stirred her heart, but she didn't know why.
She had never seen such a treasure before,
and so she began to search in hopes of finding more.

Tide after tide, her search continued. And as the tides changed, so did Theta.

Many waves and many kinds of creatures passed.
So many, for so long, that she now was beginning to look like one of them.

Her long finlike tail was her only notice to the passing of time.

Hollow-hearted and searching, she swam and swam
down into the very dark depths of the blue.
It was there, in the still of the silent blue, that she found something...

It was her slipper.

The sight of the slipper lit her heart,
just as the first treasure did, but again she did not know why.
She had long forgotten about her lost slipper and all that came before.
When she reached to pick it up, it began glowing a magical green light.

Suddenly, she remembered that she had seen this green light before,
many tides ago, beaming from above, upon her first found treasure.

And in that moment, Theta dreamt a sleepless dream,
as images of another Theta danced in the glow of the green.
From buried within her arose a restless rattle
that sent her heart on a bewildering battle.
Stay within the known of the blue or follow the unknown green light anew.

Into the unknown she decided to go,
and said goodbye to the blue world below.
But did the blue have to be so cruel,
to keep not only her time but her tail and footsteps too?
Crawling onto the green, her tears began to swell
as she realized a stride-less journey may not go so well.
But before she allowed sorrow to become a close friend,
a giant creature appeared and said...

"Don't cry, traveler. I will carry you home,
until the end of time, as far as I can go."

And so she found a treasure of a different kind.
One that gave her heart wings and expanded her mind,
up up and away beyond the world of time.

A treasure to last far and wide,
one never to be lost that had always been hiding inside.
One to be found wherever she chose to dwell,
even while falling or sitting still.
At last her searching heart was now at rest,
and instead she soared to the rhythm resounding from her chest.

Epilogue

Joyfully soaring, without longing, without desire, simply existing in all her glory
as she feels you searching for her, patiently waiting for you to find her,
knowing very well that day may never come. But if and when it does,
you will find she has been with you all along, in all her beauty and splendor,
waiting with open arms to catch you as you fall.

All artwork is inspired by real life events
with each individual painting containing a story of its own.
Created from 2017-2021 in no specific order without prior planning of Theta's story.

Once the final painting was complete, Theta's story developed.

ORIGINAL TITLES OF ARTWORK

Page 2 - Sinking Empire, 2017

Page 4 - Lost Love, 2017

Page 6 - Commissioned Mural, 2018

Page 8 - The Gift, 2017

Page 10 - Change of Tides, 2017

Page 12 - Found Dreams, 2017

Page 14 - The Magic Slipper, 2017

Page 16 - Hall of Mirrors, 2017

Page 18 - Goddess Rising, 2018

Page 20 - Divine Support, 2021

Page 22 - Home at Last, 2018

Page 24 - Good Night From The Other Side, 2017

1

www.ingramcontent.com/pod-product-compliance
Lightning Source LLC
LaVergne TN
LVHW072306070526
838201LV00099B/287